BACKSTREET BOYS

THE ILLUSTRATED STORY

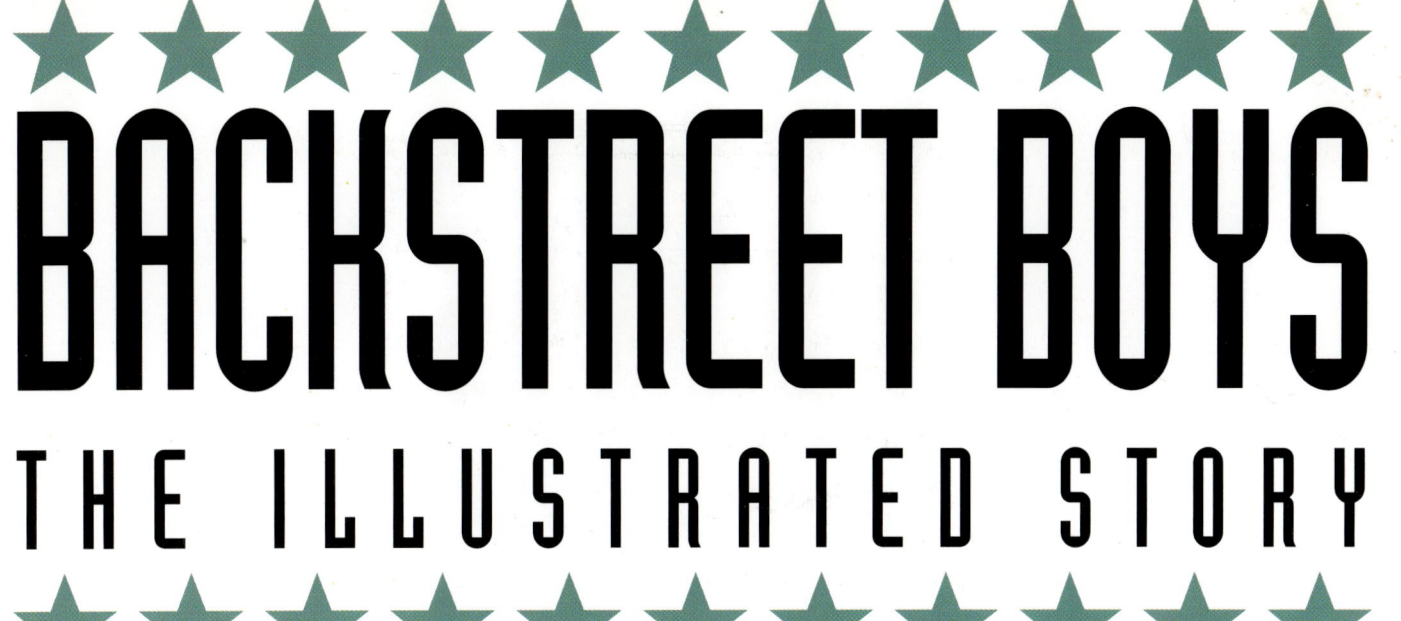

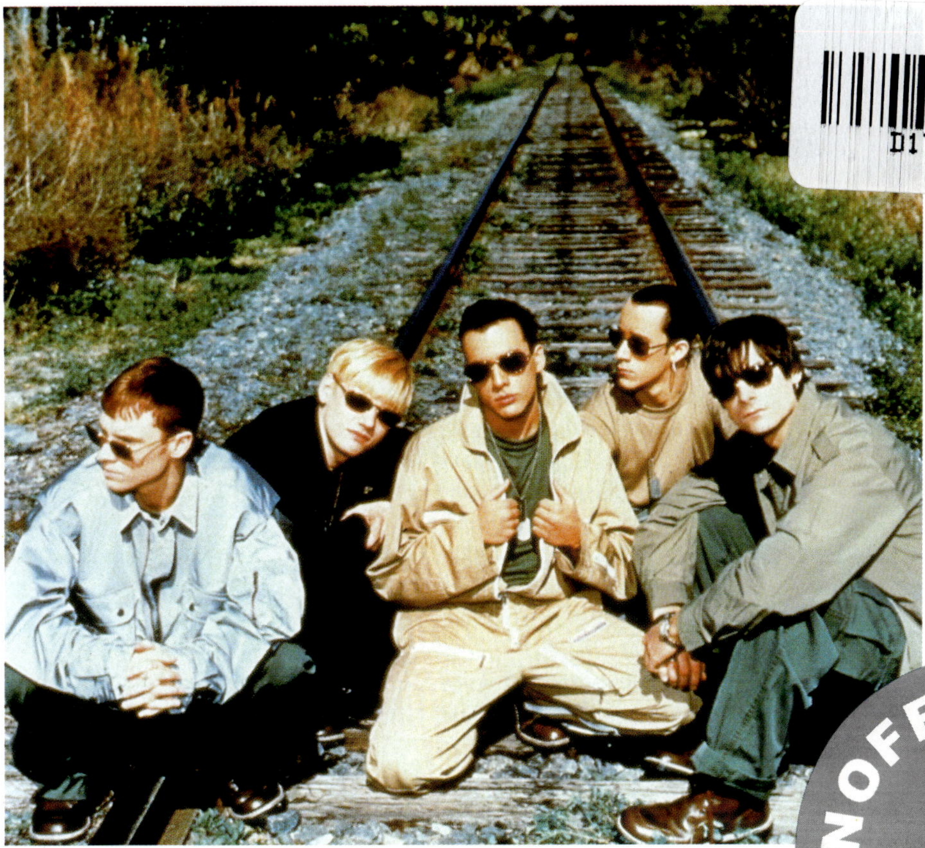

THE UNOFFICIAL BOOK

SAM HUGHES

BILLBOARD
BOOKS

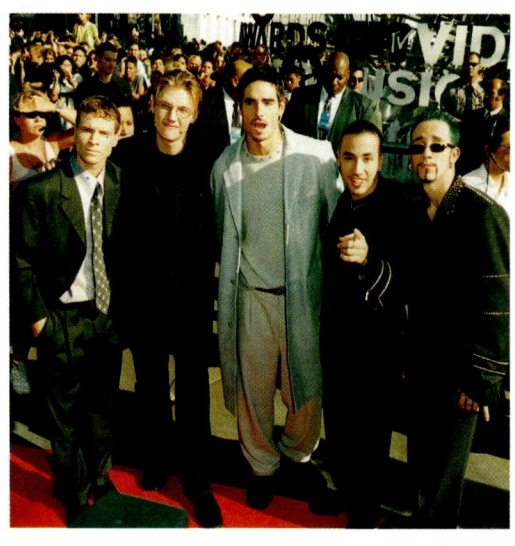

Created in 2000 by
Virgin Books
An imprint of
Virgin Publishing Ltd
Thames Wharf Studios
Rainville Road
London
W6 9HA

Copyright © 2000 Virgin Publishing Ltd
Copyright in design and layout © Virgin Publishing Ltd
Text by Sam Hughes

First published in the United States in 2000 by Billboard Books,
an imprint of Watson-Guptill Publications, a division of BPI Communications Inc.,
770 Broadway, New York, NY 10003
www.watsonguptill.com

Library of Congress Cataloging in Publication data can be obtained from the Library of Congress.
Library of Congress Card Number: 00-107464
ISBN 0-8230-7863-9

Printed and bound in Spain by Bookprint, S.L., Barcelona
Typeset in Frutiger Bold
Colour Origination by Colourwise Ltd
Designed by Stonecastle Graphics Ltd

First printing 2000

1 2 3 4 5 6 7 8 9/08 07 06 05 04 03 02 01 00

This book is not sponsored or authorized by, or affiliated in any way with Backstreet Boys
or any of its members.

Picture Credits
All Action: A. Ferr 28, John Gladwin 24, J.K. 4, 12, Chris Mackie 3, Doug Peters 9, 19, Phil Ramey 11, 32,
Paul Smith 2, S. Trupp 7, Suzan 14; Alpha: 25, 29, Mark Allan 15, 17; Corbis: Frank Ross 5, 13; Famous
Hubert Boesl 6, 8; Kurt Krieger 22; Globe Photos: Nina Prommer 23; South Beach Photo Agency: 1, 18, 21,
26, 30; Pierre ZonZon 10; Starfile: Todd Kaplan 31, Gene Shaw 27

Contents

Introduction

A long line of more than 100 girls waits patiently outside an ordinary office building in a suburb of Stockholm, Sweden. Though it may not look much from the outside, this is Cheiron Studios, the base of super-successful pop producer Max Martin.

THE GIRLS are dedicated Backstreet Boys fans from all over Europe who have heard, mostly via the Internet, that members of the Backstreet Boys will be in this studio working on their next album during July 2000. The fans have been waiting for several hours, and as time goes by the line grows longer and longer. With a mixture of excitement and anticipation, those at the front of the line pass reassuring messages back to their friends: something will happen soon…

After a while a door opens and out steps a smiling Brian Littrell, taking a break from recording. A perfect gentleman, he moves along the line of ecstatic fans signing CD covers and posters. Soon Kevin Richardson emerges to do the same, stopping to chat with fans and accepting their gifts with an easy grace. After an hour the boys have had a word with nearly everyone, and take their leave with a wave and a smile.

What is it that makes the Backstreet Boys' fans among the most dedicated and passionate in the music world? Is it the Boys' charming, lovable personalities, or their captivating, harmony-laden hits? Or is it a little bit of both? Whether you've just discovered the music of the fantastic five or consider yourself the world's biggest Backstreet Boys fan, you'll be sure to love them even more after reading this book!

Chapter One 1

No One Else Comes Close

When the Backstreet Boys' second album, *Millennium*, was released on 18 May 1999, the reaction across the world was nothing short of incredible.

FANS QUEUED all night outside record stores to be the first to buy it, radio stations had to abandon phone-in competitions to win copies as their systems crashed under the volume of calls, and many stores sold out their entire stock in the first day. In its first month of release, sales of *Millennium* reached an astonishing ten million worldwide, and the album went platinum in 25 countries across Europe, the Americas and the Far East.

But where did this success story begin? Every fan can tell you that the Backstreet Boys first started to make sweet music together in Orlando, Florida. But the seeds from which the band grew were planted in other places across the USA many years earlier.

Alex 'A.J.' McLean was born in Palm Beach, Florida, an only child who was brought up from the age of four by his mother Denise after her divorce from his father Bob. Perhaps because he was raised as the only boy in a household of women, A.J. grew up thoughtful, romantic and very much at ease in female company. Little A.J. showed huge talent for singing and dancing from an early age, stealing the show in his very first role at the age of seven – playing Dopey in a school performance of *Snow White and the Seven Dwarves*. He took classes in singing, acting and dancing as well as the regular school subjects, and his hard work was rewarded by several appearances on TV shows.

When auditioning in the Orlando area, A.J. would often run into Howard Dorough – known as Howie D or Sweet D to his hordes of adoring fans. No wonder, as this good-natured charmer certainly doesn't need to take sugar in his coffee – he's sweet enough already!

In its first month of release, sales of *Millennium* reached an astonishing ten million worldwide.

As the youngest of five siblings, Howie was supported by his large family in everything he did. No wonder he has great confidence and a wonderfully friendly personality. Prompted by his sister Polly Anna, Howie started acting at an early age, appearing with her in a production of *The Wizard of Oz*. Soon bigger and better roles followed, and by age 14 Howie was an experienced actor, with appearances in the movies *Parenthood* and *Cop and a Half* to his credit. Howie was equally talented as a singer, and discovered early on that he was blessed with the great falsetto voice that you can hear on many of the Backstreet Boys' hits today.

waterskier, Nick is never happier than when he is on top of – or beneath – the waves.

During 1993 the talented trio of Nick, Howie and A.J. hung out together during auditions, filling in spare time by harmonizing old hit songs by groups such as The Temptations. Meanwhile, the management team of Donna and Johnny Wright, who had been responsible for the worldwide success of New Kids On The Block a few years earlier, were auditioning for a new bunch of boys to sign to their associate Louis Pearlman's record label. The three guys immediately impressed the Wrights and Pearlman, who suggested that the group's sound needed to be filled out with two more singers.

Kevin Richardson, the fourth singer to join the guys, came from Lexington, Kentucky. He has often described his childhood years as idyllic. Kevin's father ran a summer camp in the Appalachian mountains, and the young Mr Richardson had the run of the place during the off-season. It was here that he first discovered his gift for music, singing in church and learning to play the piano. Naturally mature and full of confidence, Kevin knew that he had to use his God-given talent to entertain others. After appearing on stage in local musicals, and teaching ballroom dancing for a while, Kevin realized that to make it in the entertainment industry he would have to move to the big city – Orlando, Florida. Kevin had heard about the group on the Orlando grapevine, and he was thrilled

Another regular on the audition circuit was a blond bombshell named Nick Carter. He was a little younger than the other guys but equally talented. Nick was born in upstate New York, where his parents helped to run a small bar called the Yankee Rebel. As a toddler, little Nick loved to hit the dance floor and shake his stuff, which may explain his fantastic confidence on stage today! When Nick was six, his family moved to the Tampa Bay area in Florida, where he discovered his other great love besides music – the beach! An avid surfer, scuba diver and to be accepted by the younger guys as a fourth member. But the band still needed a fifth voice. And what a voice that turned out to be!

As every Backstreet fan knows, Brian Littrell is Kevin's cousin, another Lexington, Kentucky local with a natural gift for music. A soloist in his church choir from the age of just six, Brian was lucky to have an inspirational voice teacher, Barry Turner, who introduced him the work of soul legends such as Luther Vandross and encouraged him to develop his talent to the full. At the age of 18 Brian had planned to take up a musical scholarship at the University of Cincinnati, but that was all changed by one phone call from his cousin Kevin. Pulled out of his history class by an urgent request from Orlando asking him to come and audition, Brian jumped at the chance to pursue his dreams of a singing career.

Kevin knew that he had to use his God-given talent to entertain others.

Now there were five. But these would-be superstars still had work to do. They came up with a name – Backstreet Boys – inspired by the local Backstreet Market, an Orlando landmark. Now they had to get themselves noticed by a record label, so while their management bombarded record company bosses with tapes,

They couldn't go out in public in Germany for fear of being mobbed.

photos and promises that the band was hot, the Backstreet Boys were performing just about anywhere they could: schools, outdoor fairs, theme parks – a far cry from the huge arenas that now stage their sell-out shows. Eventually the hard work paid off. The band built up a dedicated following among Florida teens who knew a good thing when they saw it. Eventually the Boys signed to Jive records, who gave them their first shot at stardom with the release of 'We've Got It Goin' On' in October 1995.

Strangely though, the boys would have to tread a roundabout route before they could taste success in their own country.

The single didn't set the charts alight in the US, but German and British teenagers were quick to pick up on the fresh sound, so different from the grunge and gangsta rap that had lately been America's main musical export. For a while the guys toured Europe, building up a fanatical following and releasing two albums. It finally got to the stage that they couldn't go out in public in Germany for fear of being mobbed, but could hang out totally unnoticed in the USA.

It didn't take long for music fans Stateside to realize what they were missing. The Boys released their first US album, *Backstreet Boys*, in August 1997. It contained the best tracks from their European releases plus some new material. The killer single 'Quit Playin' Games (With My Heart)' became a huge US hit, reaching number two in the *Billboard* Hot 100. It started an avalanche of adulation. The next three singles

rocketed into the Top Ten and got the guys' pictures on a million bedroom walls across America.

Backstreet Boys went on to sell more than 28 million copies around the world, going gold or platinum in no fewer than 45 countries. Happily the Boys have always been really modest about their success, preferring to count smiling faces at their shows rather than record sales. Brian confides that as long as they can continue to make great music and please the people who matter – their fans – they will be happy.

On Top of the World

After the incredible success of *Backstreet Boys*, the guys were keen to prove that it wasn't a fluke. They wanted to produce a second album that would delight their fans, get rave reviews and showcase each of the Boys' special talents.

MILLENNIUM WAS released in May 1999. Its 12 tracks included collaborations with some of the world's most respected producers and songwriters, including Robert 'Mutt' Lange, husband of Shania Twain and producer of hit albums by artists such as Bryan Adams and Def Leppard. as well as Swedish pop maestro Max Martin. Four of the songs were co-written by members of the band. Brian contributed 'The Perfect Fan', 'The One' and the single 'Larger Than Life', while Kevin co-wrote the love song 'Back To Your Heart' with longtime BSB collaborator Gary Baker.

The album made headlines as fans snapped up a record 1.13 million copies in its first week of release – more than many groups sell in their entire careers. Music critics, who had written off the band as just another plastic pop outfit, were forced to eat their words, and reviewers praised *Millennium* as a pop masterpiece. A.J., Kevin, Brian, Nick and Howie had finally silenced their critics and they loved it – now they really were on top of the world!

Reviewers praised *Millennium* as a pop masterpiece.

Adoring Backstreet Boys fans who had made *Millennium* such a smash were now desperate to see the Boys in the flesh. And the guys were happy to oblige – they love performing live because it gives them the chance to give something back to their fans in return for their support. The *Into The Millennium* tour opened with a two-month European leg beginning in Ghent, Belgium on 2 June 1999 and continuing through Germany, the Netherlands, France, Britain, Switzerland, Italy, Spain, Norway, Finland and Sweden. European fans had been the first to succumb to Backstreet mania, but they had not had a chance to see the Boys live since the *Backstreet Boys* tour of 1997. Now they were in for a treat!

With mounting competition from other boy bands such as 'N Sync and 98 Degrees, plus a new wave of girl superstars like Britney Spears and Christina Aguilera snapping at their heels, the Backstreet Boys were under pressure to come up with something extra special for this tour. The most obvious innovation was the staging – in every arena the band performed 'in the round' on a circular stage in the middle of the arena. This allowed the guys to get close to all the fans in the auditorium, creating an intimate atmosphere in even the biggest venue.

They also got to make probably the most spectacular entrance to a concert ever. As the lights dimmed and audience expectation rose to fever pitch, the theme from *Star Wars* rang out. As if by magic Nick, Kevin, A.J., Howie and Brian appeared high in the roof of the building suspended by wires, and they seemed to fly down onto the stage on electric blue mini-surfboards. Amazing!

Wowing the crowd with ten dancers, spectacular pyrotechnics, a mind-blowing light show and lots of costume changes, the show included performances of all the Boys' biggest hits, including a funked-up 'As Long As You Love Me' and 'Everybody (Backstreet's Back)' which featured a mock thunderstorm. The Boys also performed the songs they had co-written. In a tender moment, Kevin sang 'Back To Your Heart' seated at a white grand piano, while Brian dedicated his tune 'The Perfect Fan' to mothers everywhere.

The European shows got rave reviews, and the Internet buzzed as

excited fans shared stories about the concerts with fellow fanatics around the globe. Following the phenomenal success of *Millennium* in the States, there was huge demand for tickets for the US leg of the tour. On 14 August 1999, 765,000 tickets for 39 scheduled shows went on sale. Fans queued for hours in the pouring rain to get hold of the precious tickets, booking agencies were inundated with calls and within just one hour the tour was a sell-out. The band had to schedule a further 13 shows to meet the unprecedented demand, and these also sold out immediately.

The Internet buzzed as excited fans shared stories about the concerts with fellow fanatics around the globe.

15

Due to the immense demand for tickets, some unscrupulous 'scalpers' bought up hundreds on the day they went on sale so that they could sell them illegally to desperate fans at inflated prices on the evening of the concert. The Backstreet Boys do all they can to keep ticket prices down so all their fans can afford to see them, and they hate it when these scalpers take advantage of their dedicated young fans. When they discovered that 1,200 tickets for one show had ended up in the hands of scalpers, the Boys felt so bad that their fans were being ripped off that they arranged for $75,000 to be donated to the Columbine High School benefit fund.

The US leg of the *Into The Millennium* tour was scheduled to start in Fort Lauderdale, Florida on 14 September 1999. It was to have been the perfect homecoming show for the Florida five, and fans had been gearing up to welcome them back in spectacular fashion. Unfortunately, in the week before the concert Hurricane Floyd struck the Caribbean area, and the forecast was that it would soon hit the Florida coast. The Backstreet Boys had no choice but to postpone their initial shows until later in the year. The tour eventually kicked off in Charlotte, North Carolina, but the Boys kept their promise to their Florida fans, returning in December to an ecstatic home crowd.

The *Into The Millennium* tour wowed American audiences just as it had thrilled those in Europe. It visited more than 50 cities across North America. After the final dates in Canada in March 2000, the Boys needed a break, and they headed home to rest, relax and refocus their energies after perhaps the greatest and most exhausting year of their lives.

They headed home to rest, relax and refocus their energies after perhaps the greatest and most exhausting year of their lives.

Chapter Three 3
Boys to Men

They may be adored by millions of fans and they may sell millions of records, but each of the Backstreet Boys is, at heart, just a regular guy. And just like you and I, the Backstreet Boys have had to face challenges, both in their personal and professional lives.

EACH OF them has changed in his own way since the group first got together, but rest assured that Brian, Kevin, Howie, A.J. and Nick are still as hardworking, cute and humorous as they always were.

Charming, funny and courteous, Brian Littrell works as hard as a performer in public as he does on his songwriting skills in private. As many Backstreet fans know,

Brian was diagnosed with a heart defect at an early age, a condition which eventually led to open-heart surgery in 1998. Brian made a swift recovery after the operation, but the experience taught him a few lessons. He realized that he had been taking his health for granted, dedicating his life to his career at the expense of having fun and looking after himself. At the end of 1998 the Boys signed a deal with a new management company which gave them more control over their schedules for the first time. This meant that Brian could spend more time with the people he cared about most – his family and friends.

Brian also found the opportunity to spend time with one special person: his fiancée, actress Leighanne Wallace. Brian and Leighanne met when she was an extra in the video for 'As Long As You Love Me' and romance blossomed whenever the busy pair could find some time to be together. They got engaged at Christmas 1999, when Brian was staying with Leighanne's parents for the holiday season. He popped the question right in front of her folks, and presented the lucky lady with a 24-carat diamond ring. Whatever the future may bring, you can be sure that this romantic and thoughtful guy will live his life to the full and make the most of every day.

Mature and ambitious Kevin Richardson also found happiness in his love life in 2000, marrying his long-time girlfriend Kristin Willits in June. Naturally the rest of the Backstreet Boys attended the wedding ceremony in Lexington, Kentucky, before the happy pair jetted off to the Italian island of Capri for a romantic honeymoon. Although some Backstreet fans were upset to hear that their fave guy was settling down with his sweetheart, most kind-hearted fans who e-mailed the group's website wished Kevin and Kristin a long and happy marriage.

Kevin has always had an unshakeable vision of how the Backstreet Boys' career should develop, and watching the band scale the heights they have conquered in the past two years has been his dream come true. He confesses that he sometimes gets overcome with emotion when he sees audiences singing along to Backstreet Boys songs, and he realizes just how far the group have come.

Sweet and confident Howie Dorough has always been the most approachable and chatty member of the Backstreet Boys. But this positive guy was badly brought down by the death of his sister Caroline from lupus in 1998. Lupus is a rare disease that affects a person's immune system. While it can often be successfully treated, there is no known cure. The ordeal brought him closer to his family, and Howie set up a charitable foundation in his sister's name.

When he's in party mood, Howie can still be found checking out the club scene wherever he goes, tearing it up on the dance floor with his partner-in-crime, A.J. You can be sure that Howie will always be looking super-sharp, as this dude likes to keep up with the latest fashion trends – without slavishly following them, of course.

Watching the band scale the heights they have conquered in the past two years has been Kevin's dream come true.

22

So is Howie going to follow the Kentucky cousins and get himself hitched? Relax, girls! Not any time soon. Although he has been linked with several ladies on a casual basis, Howie is still officially single – and looking! He says that he wants to find someone who will love him for who he is deep down – not just because he's one of the Backstreet Boys. With a personality like Howie's, the right girl shouldn't be difficult to find!

A.J. is also a single guy at the moment. This romantic, funny flirt is very fond of female company, but despite a few flings he is still looking for the love of his life. In the past few years Mr Chameleon has changed his hair style as often as his shirt. This guy likes to stand out from the crowd. A.J. has kept close to his mother Denise throughout his career, and when he's away on tour he really misses her home-cooked meals. When he's on the road, A.J.'s idea of a great meal out is a trip to McDonald's, so watch out girls, that's where you could end up on a date with A.J.!

23

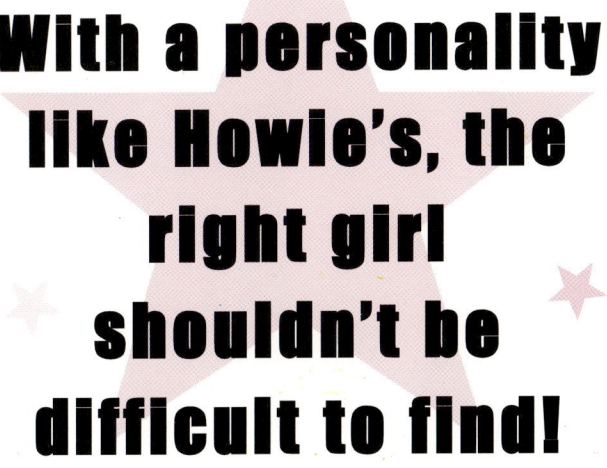

With a personality like Howie's, the right girl shouldn't be difficult to find!

The baby of the band, Nick Carter, has definitely changed the most in his years with the group, but that's because he was just 12 when the guys first got together. For one thing, from being the smallest of the five and the one most likely to get picked on, he's shot up to 6' 2"! He's also become much more independent of his family, setting up home in a house near the ocean with his five dogs and a giant plastic palm tree.

Personality-wise Nick has a touching boy-next-door humility about him. He still thinks his ears stick out too much despite all the adulation this blue-eyed babe attracts. He isn't into playing video games as much as he used to be, preferring right now to concentrate on his music. Just for fun he performs with a local band in the Florida area, and he has helped out his siblings Aaron and Leslie by penning songs for them.

On the romance front, Nick says that the perfect girl for him is someone with a love of nature, a warm personality and the patience to deal with his crazy schedule. He admits that he has been seeing a certain young lady for a while,

but he won't say any more about her except that she doesn't work in the entertainment industry.

Life as a Backstreet Boy must be strange enough to warp anyone's sense of reality. But the Boys have managed to keep their feet on the ground remarkably well. They know how lucky they are to have achieved such success. Each of them is proud to give up time and money to benefit a good cause.

The charity that Howie helped set up, the Caroline Dorough-Cochran Memorial Lupus Foundation, funds research into finding a cure for the disease. Howie recently threw a benefit party and auction for the Foundation at Universal Studios in Orlando, Florida. The most popular item to be auctioned was a dinner date with Howie himself, and it was claimed by two women who between them donated over $30,000 for the privilege.

While Brian was in hospital recovering from his heart operation, fans wishing to send him presents and flowers were encouraged to send donations instead to the Brian Littrell Healthy Heart Club for Kids, a charity which helps children recuperating from heart surgery. Brian takes a keen interest in its work, and often helps publicize the cause at public events around the country.

The Backstreet Boys are also enthusiastic supporters of the Make a Wish Foundation, a charity which makes wishes of terminally ill children come

true. In 1999 the Boys welcomed many kids backstage during their tour, and they continue to help the Foundation whenever they can.

Individually, and as a group, these caring guys are involved with many other charities and foundations. It's their way of fulfilling their promise to give something back to the young people who have given them the chance to live out their dreams.

25

Each of them is proud to give up time and money to benefit a good cause.

Chapter Four 4

Jive Talkin'

What could possibly top the incredible success the Backstreet Boys have already achieved? And what does the future hold for these hard-working and talented superstars?

WELL, EACH of the Boys has been pursuing solo projects, while also working on material for the follow-up to the mega-selling *Millennium*. The new album is still shrouded in secrecy, but A.J. has hinted in interviews that the Backstreet Boys' new sound will be innovative and fresh, containing elements of R&B, hip hop and rock, and maybe even a dash of country.

Tentatively entitled *Jive*, the album will feature collaborations with well-known songwriters, including Desmond Child and Max Martin, as well as contributions from each of the band members who continue to become more involved with production and songwriting. In the summer of 2000 the Boys took themselves off to a remote Caribbean island studio, with just a couple of engineers along to help with the equipment, so that they could concentrate on writing songs together away from the distractions of their everyday lives. Let's hope they managed to drag themselves away from the beach and into the studio!

Individually, each of the guys has been devoting time and effort to his own creative projects, both as part of and separate from the group. Howie has been writing with legendary R&B producer Babyface, and has set up his own production company, the snappily named 'Howie Do It', to discover and develop new artists. The company's first signing is Howie's sister Polly Anna, whose debut album is currently in production. It will include a duet with none other than Howie himself.

Each of the guys has been devoting time and effort to his own creative projects.

Kevin and Brian have both been focusing on their songwriting skills in the past year. Kevin has set up a studio in his home, and has been working with a number of co-writers on possible songs for the new album. He and Brian joined the other guys in Sweden in July 2000 to begin recording new tracks with collaborator Max Martin. While they were there, they found themselves sharing a studio and a hotel with Irish boy band Westlife. The bands have a lot of mutual respect for one another's work, and they all were happy to provide autographs for fans who had camped out in the city in the hope of meeting their idols. Another visitor to the Stockholm studio was Crown Princess Victoria of Sweden, who made a secret and unofficial visit to hang out with the band for a few hours. It seems Britney Spears isn't the only artist to have a royal fan!

A.J. seems to have a burning desire to make as much music as he can! As well as his contributions to the new BSB album, and a tentative plan for a solo R&B release, he is also putting a lot of energy into the performances of his alter ego, Johnny No-Name. Taking on the identity of a wild British rock singer brought up in Memphis, Tennessee, A.J. has been able to kick it up live and

express the 'rockier' side of his nature, performing covers of songs by the likes of Rage Against the Machine and Stone Temple Pilots. As Johnny No-Name, A.J. has played several charity concerts in small venues in the Midwest to benefit VH1's Save the Music Foundation, which helps fund music classes in public schools across America.

Nick also has a pet project: managing a band in the Tampa Bay area called Born Into Chaos. When the group played a small local venue in June 2000, Backstreet Boys fans in the audience were amazed to see Nick himself join in, first on drums and then on lead vocals, performing a number of tracks including James Brown's 'I Feel Good'.

As well as contributing songs to the Backstreet Boys albums, Brian has been pursuing his ambition of writing material for other artists. A song Brian has penned for fellow Jive Records artist Don Phillip entitled 'How Did I Ever' is slated to be released as Don's second single.

A.J. seems to have a burning desire to make as much music as he can!

While in Europe they ran into soul legend Lionel Richie, and collaborated with him on a track called 'Cinderella' on his latest album *Renaissance.*

Brian has also become involved in the movies, producing and co-starring in an independently made film called *Olive Juice*. A release date has not yet been set for the film, which features Brian in a cameo role as a carriage driver, as well as appearances by his fiancée Leighanne and fellow BSB A.J.

In late July 2000 Brian and Leighanne were pretty upset when their beloved chihuahuas, Tyke and Litty, were dognapped, apparently by over-zealous fans. An appeal was posted on the Boys' official website along with the offer of a substantial reward, and within days the dogs were returned to their rightful and relieved owners.

The Backstreet Boys as a group enjoy working with artists they admire when they get a chance. While in Europe they ran into soul legend Lionel Richie, and collaborated with him on a track called 'Cinderella' on his latest album *Renaissance*. And, taking a break from work on their album in Sweden, the Boys popped over to London's Hyde Park to appear with Elton John at the annual Party in the Park on 9 July 2000. The Boys were sadly without A.J., who had returned to the US to spend time with his sick grandfather. The four guys accompanied Elton John on two songs, before E.J. stood in for A.J. on the Boys' tracks 'The One' and 'I Want It That Way'.

Each of the Boys is transformed into a superhero with his own special power.

It's no secret that Nick loves comic books and drawing cartoons, and for years he has sketched himself and the other guys as comic book characters during quiet times on tour. His dreams came true early in 2000 when the Backstreet Boys teamed up with artist Stan Lee to create a comic book based on the Boys. In *The Backstreet Boys Project* each of the Boys is transformed into a superhero with his own special power – their mission is to save the Earth from alien attack.

The comic book is available through the band's official website, and is sure to win the guys a few more male fans attracted by their cool comic book capers.

Whatever new opportunities and challenges the future holds for the Backstreet Boys, you can be sure that these born entertainers will go on developing as artists, giving their all for their fans and winning respect in tomorrow's music world. We can't wait!